FRANK HERNANDEZ

# A Life
# REDEEMED

## FROM GANGS, TO PRISON, TO THE PULPIT

Published by Eagle's Wings Press

Design and editorial support by:
EVANGELISTA MEDIA & CONSULTING
Via Maiella, 1 66020 San Giovanni Teatino (CH) – Italy
publisher@evangelistamedia.com
www.evangelistamedia.com

For Worldwide Distribution, Printed in the USA.

1 2 3 4 5 6 / 22 21 20 19

# DEDICATION

First, this book is for the glory and honor of my Lord and Savior Jesus Christ. Without You in my life, none of this is possible.

I also dedicate this book to my beautiful wife, Brenda, and our children, Andrea, Jeanette and my son-in-love Gilzy, my son Frank Jr. and my daughter-in-love Nena, and my son Albert. To all our grandchildren, my mom Martha Flores and dad Rudy Flores, my brothers Rudy, Robert, Angel, Tony, my sisters Christina and Sarah, and my entire family.

And to my amazing church family at Kingdom Living—you have inspired me in so many ways.

# Acknowledgments

I have mentors in my life that I acknowledge with love because they helped me become the man I am today:

Pastors Ron and Debra Friese, who mentored me while I was in prison.

Pastors Kurt and Mary Schroeder, who saw the anointing upon my wife, Brenda, and I and pushed us to become who we are today. You became spiritual parents to us and helped us run to the prize of Christ.

Carlos and Claudia Mongello, who took a chance on me when no else would. You have truly been a blessing and have pushed and stretched me to see the Kingdom of God like I have never seen it before.

Dean and Lisa Romesburg, who have loved us since day one. Your lives have truly reflected the heart of God to me. You have inspired me to love despite what I see.

Dr. Dennis Sempebwa, you have truly been a key to opening my eyes and heart to what Jesus has in store for Brenda and me. You challenged me and have truly become more than a mentor. You have also become a spiritual papa to us. There are no words to express my gratitude and love for you.

# CONTENTS

## Chapter 1

# PRISON IT IS!

It was in the early part of January 2004, I was in a jail cell, nervous and unsure of my fate. As I laid on my bed in the cold jail cell, all I could think of was how my family would be without me. How was my wife and kids going to handle life without me being there, to provide for them? I couldn't sleep.

As the morning dawned to reflect a new day, I could hear the correctional officers arriving to start their shift. Soon they would awaken me to get up so I could appear in court to face the judge and hear my sentence.

As I walked through the underneath corridors that connected the jail and the court house in Riverside, California, I came across some of the homies from my barrio (gang members from a Spanish-speaking neighborhood). As we greeted one another with a simple head nod, all that went through my mind was wondering how long my life would continue in this whirlwind of chaos. I replayed the night I got caught up that put me in this place. I had replayed it over and over. If only I would have done something different, if only I would've done this or that.

This turmoil was something I was very familiar with. I had grown up in the juvenile criminal system from the age of twelve—and every time I got caught, I would replay the choices I made that brought me to where I ended up.

Now as an adult, it had been awhile since I had been in this predicament. But once again, here I was ready to face the judge and the district attorney—the very same who had previously given me a break by not sentencing me to prison a few months back. Now they would be seeing me again for the same crime. I knew that I would be going away for some prison time in a state facility this time around.

As I sat in the courtroom, I saw case after case being called up. I could hear the judge give prison time to every inmate facing him. Soon it would be my turn. As my time came up to be sentenced, I had said a little prayer hoping for the best. Then I heard the judge declare my fate, five years in the California prison system. I took a deep breath and wondered how I was going to tell my wife that I was going away for five years.

Later in the day after I was sentenced and had walked back to my jail cell, so many thoughts were racing through my mind. All I could think about was my wife and kids.

I began to do the math—my kids would be this age and that age when I would be released and return home.

Then something began to tug at my heart—a sudden peace came over me. It began to shake me in the core of my being. I couldn't understand it; one minute prior to that coming over me, my mind was racing with craziness, then BAM! I could feel the peace of God flood my thoughts.

It was time to call my wife and deliver the news of my sentence. I made the call home, and we made some small talk about her day's events at home. Then came the question, "What happened at court?" I told her I was sentenced to five years in prison. She began to cry and asked me what the heck was she supposed to do. She believed I was coming home, and now she had to face the fact that I was going to be gone for five years. When we ended the phone call, she was still really upset that I was going away for so long.

The homies in my unit were talking about their sentencing, and we all were trying to be tough, not allowing the reality of our sentencing to affect us—but deep down I could sense that life was about to take a whole new turn for me.

You see, I had grown up in the system as a juvenile, as I mentioned before. However, as an adult I had not done any serious time. In fact, this was really my first time going to prison. So now I was facing the reality of my sentence. I figured I would leave my family life in the back of my mind, as I began to come to the realization that I would soon be in a prison yard. I would have to be tough and not show any weakness. The mindset of my youth began to come back to me. I would do what I had to do to survive in that prison yard. Little did I know that going into prison would change my life forever.

Here is my story.

# Chapter 2

# LIFE BEGINS

The year was 1970 and my family life was being shaking up as my mother announced that she was going to have a baby. Back then it was uncommon for a young lady to have a baby out of wedlock, let alone a young lady who was still in high school. My mother met my father after he got out of prison. There is no love story that unfolded between the two; as a matter of fact, after I was born my parents didn't stay together, and I ended up being raised by my mother, stepfather, and my maternal grandparents.

When the time came for me to enter this world, things had settled down around my grandparents' home. In fact, they were excited to have another baby in the house. When my mother brought me home, I became the favorite of the household. I could do no wrong in the eyes of Grandpa Alfred. My mother's siblings were all still living at home; so now with me in the home, I was like the new little brother to them. In fact, my grandpa became so overprotective of me, that my mother couldn't do anything to me, without his approval.

My biological father's name was Tony. He was known as "Beaver" in the neighborhood. He had grown up fighting, using drugs, and getting into trouble. From juvenile hall all the way to prison. To this day, I still don't know too much about his family or how the separation from me affected him. About a month before he was killed, I met up with him, which I will get into later in the book.

It's strange to me that my biological father, who lived in the same little town as my mother and I, never came into contact with me. At least not that I can remember or know of. When I was young, I recall several times when we would be going to a store or somewhere, and I was told to hide in the back seat of my grandparents' car because my dad was in the area looking for me. I'm not sure why I was kept from seeing my father's family, at least his parents. So much of my childhood is still a mystery to me to this day. There are just so many different stories that I don't know which is the right story to believe. All I know is that when I did eventually grow old enough to know them (my biological father's parents), they really loved me. Which is what I was always looking for.

While as my young mother and I began our life together, my mom eventually met my stepdad when I was about two years old. He ended up raising me, and is the one whom I know today as my father. Of course, I don't recall too much of their beginning love story. My stepdad was also a young man himself. So, taking on the responsibility of not only having to provide for his new love, but also for me, was, I'm sure, difficult and scary.

As my mom and new dad started their new life together, my stepdad was the total opposite of my biological father. My father had been in and out of prison, and my stepdad didn't resemble a gangster at all, although most of his brothers were from my barrio. The two hit the ground running, so to speak, and my mom quickly became pregnant with my little brother Rudy Jr. Three months after my brother was born, my mom announced to the family that she was pregnant again with my other little brother Robert. So now there were three of us little guys running all over.

My mom and dad had their hands full, so my mom would go to work and drop me off with my grandparents. As mentioned before, I became the favorite grandchild of my Grandpa Alfred. He loved me like no other. Although Grandpa did drink a lot, during those times is when he would declare his love for me. It was well known in my family that no one could tell me to do anything I didn't want to do if my grandpa was around. Even at my young age, I knew that I could have anything I wanted with him on my side, so I would use that to my advantage.

My mom's little sister, Rosie, was the youngest in the family. With me being around, I'm sure I must have stolen her rights as the youngest in the family. I received a lot of attention and was known for getting my way. Those are some great memories for me.

# Chapter 3

# GROWING PAINS

I can recall a lot of things that happened to me and things that I had witnessed as a young boy. I had experienced so much as young child. I was pretty confused at my upbringing. In one home I felt the love of my grandparents, and in my home with my mom and dad, there was some turmoil and stress. I witnessed a lot of pain and abuse growing up.

My life began to shape its course when I began to notice the difference in how I was treated in my home. My little brothers were treated like little kings, and I was like the cinder-fella of the home. My dad treated me different from my little brothers. He and my mom would argue about the way he treated me and they would end up fighting. My dad and mom were constantly arguing and eventually it became pretty abusive. I would cry and try to shelter my little brothers. I remember I would try to get them into another room, so they wouldn't have to witness the fighting. I was young, probably around six years old. They were around two and three years old.

At my grandparents' home it was the opposite, a lot of love and only a few fights when my grandpa would come home drunk. My grandmother would always tell me stories about the love of Jesus. I can recall countless times when Grandma would sit me down and pour into me about the Bible. Her dad was a pastor and she was so proud of my great-grandpa. On her side of the family there were a lot of Christians. She and her twin sister were in the church choir when they were younger. So, because I was like a son to them, she wanted to make sure that I knew about Jesus. Little did she know that the seed she planted would flourish and help me become the man I am today.

Two of my mother's sisters were still living at home with Grandma and Grandpa as well as one of my uncles. My aunt Rosie was my mother's youngest sister and we were about seven years' difference in age. When she was a teenager and wanted to go out to the movies, she would have to take me along, and my grandpa would pay me money to tell on her. I was young, so of course I would tell all that needed to be told. Rosie would get mad at me, but she couldn't do anything to me, because Grandpa would not let anyone touch me. I was a little brat in the Hernandez home.

Then came the times when I would go home to my mom and dad's house. We lived in an apartment in Corona. Things were different there; but because I couldn't compare it to anything else, I assumed that it was normal the way my dad treated me. I noticed I was being singled out and it puzzled me. It felt really strange to me. I didn't know that my stepdad was not my real father. I had grown up thinking that he was my real father, so I couldn't pinpoint why I was treated differently. All I knew was that my brothers were being loved different from the way I was loved.

As young as I was, I could notice the difference. It did something to me. It created a hunger to be loved by my father. It created an emptiness in me and made me feel like I was inadequate in who I was. Of course, at that time, I couldn't determine this need. However, looking back on my life, it was a deep desire for me to be loved by him. Every child wants to be loved by their parents. This was no different, because I was led to believe that he was my real father. The Bible states in Romans 8:28 that *"we know that in all things God works for the good of those who love him, who have been called according to his purpose."* This verse would be fulfilled in my life as you will see in my later years in life.

My other aunt, Bertha, was like a big sister to me. Throughout my young life, she had witnessed some of things done to me. She also lived with my parents later in the years, so she was my little protector. There are many memories I have of all the craziness that I was exposed to as young boy. I am grateful that the Lord always made a way of escape for me. Going from my parents' apartment to my grandparents' home was one of the ways I escaped the chaos.

My grandparents lived right in the barrio of Corona, where I had witnessed even more craziness. The neighborhood was always popping off with action. This was in the late 1970s, when the local gangs were at the prime of their days, with *Lowrider Magazine* (a magazine company that portrayed lowrider cars and gangs in the USA) coming to our barrio, and a local peace treaty with Casa Blanca, a local barrio who would later become a rival throughout my hay-days in life. We lived right across the street from all the action of it all. Corona barrio was on 4th Street in Corona, with Merrill and Sheridan streets on its East and West side.

I was always running around outside and got to know a lot of the homies from my barrio. There was a boys' club right next door to us, so during the day I would go there with all the guys. But at night I had to be inside, because at night around the barrio, it became a different neighborhood. It was so crazy that the local police would not drive through the barrio. They would use the surrounding streets (Merrill, Sheridan and 3rd Street) to patrol and put on their spotlights to survey the barrio, but never come through.

The night life in the barrio was alive with violence, drugs, and craziness. The homies from my barrio would drive through with no lights on, just the parking lights. Every car radio was blaring its oldies or funk music from inside the car. They would cruise at 5-10 mph because of all the homeboys and homegirls in the street. There would even be times when they would block off the street and have a block party. There were no rules for the gangs. Everyone was getting high and pretty much doing what they wanted. This was life in the barrio. This is where I grew up and became part of this barrio.

Even though I was exposed to a lot of craziness as a young boy, it was the love that my grandparents showed me in the middle of all the chaos that made a difference in my life. There is a Scripture in the Bible that says, *"Above all, love each other deeply, because love covers over a multitude of sins"* (1 Peter 4:8). This is something that my grandparents showed me without realizing it. In spite of all that was going on, they poured love on me. Through their display of love, I was able to manage the growing pains of life that I was experiencing as a young boy.

## Chapter 4

# MY EYES WERE OPENED

The year was 1978, and now I was eight years old. I was living with my parents on the weekends and staying with my grandparents during the week for school. Since my mom and dad both worked, my grandpa would send me to school so that my mom wouldn't have to worry about sending me off so early, as my parents both had to start work early in the morning. If I stayed with them during the week, I would've had to go to school before the sun came up. It just made sense for my grandpa to get me to school and watch after me during the week.

I can still vividly remember one weekend that would alter my life, and all that I thought it to be at eight years of age. I was going with my mother to a local 7-11 convenience store where we were going to buy milk. My mom pulled up in front of the store and asked me to get out and buy the milk. I noticed a guy looking at me the moment I walked in the store; his stare made me feel uncomfortable. The store clerk also noticed. She was one of the regular clerks who knew me, since I was in the store a lot.

As I placed the milk on the counter to pay for it, this guy asked if that's all I wanted. He went on to ask if I would like to buy some candy and ice cream. I shook my head no. The lady working behind the counter asked me, "Frankie, where's your mom?" I said, "Right there in the car," pointing toward outside. She said, "Why don't you go outside and ask her?" I believe she was trying to protect me from the guy. As I walked outside, the guy followed me; and when I went to ask my mom who was this guy, I could see my mom's expression, it was as if she had seen a ghost. She turned pale, and before she could mutter a response, the guy says he's my uncle, my mom's brother.

I stood there waiting for my mother to validate his response. She said, "Yes, he is your uncle." He dropped to a knee to look me in the eye and gave me a big hug. He said that he waited for a long time to see me. I could feel something that I had never felt stirring up in me. It was an emotion that I cannot explain. He began to smother me in kisses and asked my mom if he could take me in the store to buy me some treats. We ended up walking hand and hand into the store. I didn't know what to buy, so I picked out a few items and went back to my mom in the car. As I went to the car, my uncle opened the door for me, and said, "Frankie, you can't let your dad know that you saw me. He doesn't like me too much, and he might get mad if you tell him you saw me." I agreed and said that I wouldn't let anyone know. My mom then started the car, and as we left, he said that he would see me later.

A couple of weeks passed, and I couldn't shake the feeling I had after meeting this man; there was something different about him. My dad never spoke to me like that. I could feel his heart as he spoke. It may sound a little funny, but something touched my heart. I had desired my dad to love me like that. But for some reason, I couldn't get the attention from him that a young boy needed. It was always the opposite. I always felt like I wasn't good enough to be loved by him. As a young boy, it confused me to see him treat me like this. It was a hunger that I developed because I saw him treat my two little brothers different from me. I saw my dad love my brothers like my uncle was loving on me for that moment when I met him.

I think it was about three to four weeks later when I woke up in the middle of the night and couldn't stop crying. I was at my grandparents' home, and my grandmother was asking me what was wrong. Why was I crying? I didn't know why I was crying. I just kept saying that my heart hurt. It wasn't like a pain or anything like that, it was a deep sadness that came over me.

My grandma and grandpa couldn't get me to stop crying. I ended up crying myself to sleep. For the next couple of days, I was sad. I remember not feeling myself, it was a feeling that I can't explain. My mom came and picked me up and took me to my dad's mom's house. I remember once we got there, she took me in the back room. She sat me down, and asked me if I remember my uncle Tony. The one I met at 7-11. I nodded my head that I remembered. "Well," she says, "well, someone killed him, and he isn't your uncle, he's your dad."

Then she walked out and left me in the room. It was like a train had hit me at full steam. All my questions to why I was treated differently suddenly began to make sense. All my emotions started going crazy. I began to cry. I was so mad. My little heart was changed, and I was filled with rage. My life was suddenly changed, and all I wanted at that moment was to kill. I wanted to kill the person responsible for my dad's death. Nothing was more important for me at that time.

From that moment on, I didn't want to be a superhero, I didn't want to be a doctor, lawyer, or police officer. It was the opposite. I wanted to be a gangster and learn how to be a killer. I had witnessed enough of their lifestyle to know that being like them would get me to be the person I needed to be to fulfill my newfound goal in life. My stepdad's brothers were all homies from the barrio. I knew I had to learn from them. Being around them, I could watch and learn the lifestyle. They were well known in the barrio. There were five of them I could learn from.

All five of my uncles all loved me and had always looked out for me. I was set to watch and learn from them. They never knew that I was watching how they talked, and how they presented themselves as gangsters. It began to fascinate me how they carried themselves. It wouldn't be long till I was old enough to be like them, a real homie from the barrio. The course was set!

# Chapter 5

# BLURRED VISION

A short time later in the same year of 1978, my mom and dad purchased their first home. They let my grandparents know that I would no longer be going to live with them during the week. My parents would now have me full time. The home they purchased was far from the barrio. It was an all-white neighborhood. I remember standing in the back of the truck holding down some of the furniture—back in those days, it was legal to sit in the back of an open-bed of a pickup truck in California.

As we drove down the street to our new home, some of the neighbors were outside their homes, and I could see them pointing at us, like we were something they had never seen before. It was almost like something out of the movies. At the time, I was eight years old and had a shaved head. I didn't want to be with my parents, so I had a bad attitude. It showed on my face as we drove down the street with our belongings.

A few weeks passed, and I was adjusting to the new home, new school, and most of all living with my parents. There was a lot for me to get used to. I believe it was around this time when my dad began to reach out to me and try his best to love me. We began a new season in our relationship. Something began to click with us. We began a relationship that never existed before.

As the two of us got along better, I began to meet new friends in our new neighborhood. I found that I was really good at sports. All the neighborhood kids played baseball and football outside of our homes. The street I lived on was Cottonwood Court in Corona. There were three streets that connected to one another. My street, which was on the southside and turned into Redwood Court, swept up like a U-shape, and in the middle of the two streets was Aspen Court. Sometimes all the parents came out to watch us play. It was almost like an old 1950s TV show where everyone got along.

I ended up playing Little League Baseball and Jr. All-American Football. My dad was a big football fan, so the sports drew us pretty close. Especially because I was so good. It made him proud that the other kids' parents all were asking whose son I was, because I stood out among the other players. Of course, my mom and dad raised their hands and said, "That's our son!" My football team traveled to other cities to play, and with us driving to and from my games, my mom and dad were also growing in their relationship. It was good for the whole family.

There was no more fighting for about two years, and by this time my parents had their third child. My little brother Angel was born in August 1978. The birth of Angel brought all of us joy. He was a great addition to our family. Something was different about him—he was special. Years later my little brother Angel would pass away, which would begin a backward journey for me.

I recall that during these peaceful times in my relationship with my dad he took me for a ride and we were talking. He stopped at a signal light, and before the light turned green, he looked at me and asked me, "Frank, I want to ask you a question. How would you feel if I adopted you?" I said, "What do you mean?" He said that we would go to court so I could have the name Flores as my last name. At that moment and season in our lives, I was happy, and almost began to cry as I finally felt that I was accepted by him.

I said, "Yes, Dad, that would be awesome!" As we drove off, our eyes filled with tears of joy. A lot transpired in that year as we all seemed to be getting along. But then something changed. It seemed I had blurred vision of reality. It was the calm before the storm.

*Chapter 6*

# JESUS CALLS ME BY NAME

It was Easter of 1979, and a local church by the name of Goodnews Church led by Pastors Kurt and Mary Schroeder were putting on a live production of the life of Jesus. I was nine years old at the time, and my grandma had bought tickets for us to attend. The theater where the play was being performed was sold out. It was a local theater in town at the downtown civic center. I really didn't want to go—little did I know that seeing this play would touch me in a special way.

The play portrayed the life of Jesus, it went along with the Gospels and included the crucifixion and resurrection of Jesus. It really brought the Bible to life for me. Everything that my grandmother had told me when I was growing up was now being played out before my eyes. I was captivated as I watched the reenactments of Jesus healing the blind man and raising Lazarus from the dead. I remember sitting at the edge of my seat, my eyes fixated on the stage as each scene was played out.

As the play moved along, the time came for Jesus to be put on trial. I could hear the crowd in the play shouting to crucify Him. My eyes filled with tears as I witnessed Him heal so many people and reveal His heart of love for each of them. Now here they were yelling out to crucify the very One who loved them. I could feel my heart beating against my chest, as I knew what was coming next.

Soon the stage cleared and coming down the aisle was Jesus, followed by the Roman soldiers beating Him as He carried the Cross. This was all being played out as Pastor Mary Alice Schroeder was singing the Via Dolorosa song. As I saw the blood coming off the man who played Jesus, and the guards hitting Him, my eyes were flowing with tears, as I witnessed Him being beaten and crucified.

After watching His real-life crucifixion played out on stage, next would come His resurrection. My eyes were still filled with tears; I couldn't shake the feeling of peace that was coming over me. I sat in amazement as I watched the resurrection scene. Then the play ended and everyone in the theater stood to their feet in an eruption of applause.

Afterward, Pastor Kurt took the stage. I don't recall the exact words he spoke, I just remember running to the stage when he asked if anyone would like to come up to receive prayer or if anyone wanted to accept Jesus into their lives. I didn't even ask my grandma or hesitate, I knew that I needed Jesus. At the altar, I don't know who prayed with me, but after the prayer I remember following a team to the back of the theater and receiving more prayer and a Bible.

My grandma asked me where I went, although I'm sure she saw me run up to the altar. I told her all about the prayer and showed her my Bible. She was so very happy for me that she started to cry. It was so amazing to see that play, it really broke down some walls of hate in my life. I really felt the Lord calling my name, asking me if I will now allow Him to show me His love. As young as I was, I was a little boy of nine who was mixed up with hate but wanting most of all to be loved. I can still remember the mixed feelings that were so hard to tell anyone.

I was still playing youth football, so I was able to shift a lot of my anger onto the field. I was good, as I played both offensive and defensive sides of the field. I became known as one of the hardest hitting guys on my team. I'm really glad that I was playing football, as it helped me with a lot of my anger issues.

Soon all that would come to a close and there was no place to filter my anger. However, through it all, I still could remember the day that Jesus called me by name. It would be years later when I would go back to the church that put on the play. Little did I know that Pastors Kurt and Mary Schroeder would play a significant part in my life years later.

*Chapter 7*

# BACK TO REALITY

It was now the start of the new school year in 1981. I was ten years old, soon to be eleven the following month. I was entering the sixth grade. My parents were working their full-time jobs, and we were adjusted to our new home. My brothers and I had made new friends, and we were all known in our little community. It had helped us being good at sports, since the whole neighborhood played sports.

My mom and dad just had their last child, the one they were waiting for, my little sister Christina. After having four boys, they now had a little girl. She was the prize of our family. We were so happy to have a little sister, and we boys vowed to protect her growing up.

For the past two years, Dad had worked rotating shifts, and my mother had worked the morning shift at her job. I stayed home a lot to take care of my little brother, so I ended up missing a lot of school and got behind in my work assignments. I loved to read. I remember reading a lot of books growing up. My dad was attending college to become a police officer, so I would grab his books and read them when I stayed home.

It was about this time when things began to shift. My mom was the one who was always talking on the phone to family who would call—as well as the bill collectors. My dad never talked on the phone. One day when I stayed home from school and was passing by my parents' bedroom, I overheard my dad talking on the phone. His voice was soft and he was laughing. It was a tone that I never heard him use, not even with my mom. So, it struck me that he was talking to another lady. My dad had extramarital affairs before, so after my mom got home from work, I told her what I had heard.

It wasn't long after that when I began to feel the wrath of my dad, as he resorted to his old ways of treating me badly. Although he did hold back some; because I was a bit older now, he couldn't mistreat me too much. Nevertheless, things changed, and not for the better. Our relationship began to crumble. I recall one evening when he walked in with food for us, and as the hamburgers were passed out to my brothers, there wasn't one for me. I wasn't sure if that was intentional, but I asked, "Where's mine?"

Dad said, "You don't get one." Since I was a "rat," he gave me cheese from the refrigerator. I blew up. I was so mad. I told him, "If it isn't true that you were talking to a girl, then you wouldn't be acting this way with me. You know it's true, stop denying it!" I stormed out of the dining room and went to my room.

A few weeks later Dad would come clean to Mom and admitted the affair, which devastated my mother. Our home became a nightmare to live in. There was constant fighting between them. They would lock themselves in their room and leave us to ourselves pretty much. I ended up sometimes cooking meals for my little brothers. They were so consumed with their issues that we were pretty much on our own.

I wasn't a little boy anymore. I still was playing sports, but my parents were no longer involved as much as before. I would hitch rides with the neighbors to practices and games. It would be my last year playing sports and I began to feel that hate again—the emptiness that I had remembered from the time when my biological father had died. The last few years of happiness seemed to be a complete lie to me. My heart was filled with anger. My rage intensified, as now I was older so I understood things more clearly than I did when I was eight years old.

I decided to follow through with my original plans of hate. As the school year progressed, I would soon be in junior high. In my eyes, it was time to grow up. I was no longer a kid. I had witnessed so much in my young life, and had been through a lot for a normal eleven-year-old kid. I was really mature for my age. It was time to get back on track and learn the ways of the streets. The short-lived setback of a happy, make-believe family was over.

## Chapter 8

# JUMPED IN

It was a whole new life for me. I was now officially in junior high, a seventh grader. It was time to make my mark. I had several uncles who were from the barrio, but I didn't want the homies in school knowing that I was related to them. I wanted to make my own name, not ride on their reputation.

At the time, junior high included seventh, eighth, and ninth grades. High school in Corona was tenth through twelfth grades. So, I was going to school with a lot of older kids who knew their way around the barrio. Homies were there who were in the gangs that represented our barrio in our school. There were three different junior high schools, and the one I attended was the one where all the kids that lived in the barrio attended. So there were plenty of homies from the hood.

As I began to make friends with the homeboys, it was time to get "jumped in," a gang initiation process where some of the strongest members of the gang would beat up a young kid. One day I was in the locker room getting dressed for PE class and a couple of homies came up to me and said, "Hey, you've been hanging around us, so you need to get jumped in." They were going around jumping in a few seventh graders, so now it was my turn. I turned and said, "Yea, I want to get jumped in."

So the guys doing the fighting came at me and the fight was on. I had been taking boxing training at the local boxing club, so I was a pretty good fighter. I put up a good fight, and actually a few who witnessed the fight said I could really fight. That made me feel like I could take on the world. I was now part of the hood.

Because I lived so far from the barrio, I would get upset because all the homies were would talk at school about the parties and the things going on around the hood. I was active in the things that went on at school with the homies, but I knew that it wasn't enough. I had to be in the hood, to know what was going on at all times. As I began to contemplate my situation in my head, I settled it in my heart that I would sneak out on the weekends and go to the barrio. That's where everyone who was part of the hood hung out.

The hood was a field surrounded by four different streets. The part we all hung out on was Fourth Street. The things that happened there were so crazy that the local police wouldn't drive through the street, they would only drive on the other three streets and shine their light on us. The homeboys would shoot out the street lights and everyone going through Fourth Street would drive with only their parking lights on. It was the rules of the barrio.

So now I was sneaking out on the weekends, and walking to the barrio. It was a two-mile walk from my house to Fourth Street. I was determined to be part of the barrio. I never told any of my homies that I lived so far away. I was embarrassed that we lived in an all-white neighborhood. I didn't want the homies to think that I was some rich kid, so I never told anyone where I lived—at least not right away.

As I began to hang out more with the homies, I started using PCP. It was the drug of choice in the barrio at that time. We would use a Kool cigarette and dip it into a vanilla extract bottle containing PCP. Everyone on Fourth Street was smoking what we called super-kools, like regular cigarettes.

It was around this time when my mom took me to a house not far from where we lived and told me that my biological dad's parents lived there. I was shocked that they actually lived right down the street from us, and not once did anyone tell me. I was fuming angry, but yet happy that I finally would meet someone from his family. We knocked on the door and they immediately knew who I was. My grandma began to cry with a deep cry as she hugged me. I've been told that I look exactly like my dad, so with him being gone, I was immediately the favorite. I was mad at my mom and dad for keeping me away from my grandparents and aunts. They lived so close to us, and I never knew why they kept me from them.

I remember one time when I had stopped by my grandma and grandpa's house on the way to the barrio, and on the couch was a guy my age. He was really quiet. I nodded my head, and he waved. Just then Aunt Sandra came into the room and said to me, "Mijo, this is your cousin Roy. He is visiting us." We made some small talk and I left. A few weeks passed and my cousin Roy moved into my grandparents' home, with my other cousin Pancho, and their dad, my uncle, Roy Sr.

My cousin Roy and I became really close. He too would eventually get jumped in the barrio and the two of us began to party and hang out together. One Saturday night we both had smoked some super-kools, and I was pretty high. We got separated and I ended up walking home by myself. I don't remember too much of the night, but I do remember being stopped by the police. The officer took me in for being under the influence of PCP. That's when all my sneaking out was exposed.

The police called my mom to let her know I was in their custody. She argued with the police officer saying that I was in bed and they must have the wrong person. I remember the police looking at me and saying, "You got them fooled." My dad told my mom to go look in my room. Sure enough, it was me they had at the police station. She came down and picked me up.

Of course, the normal yelling and what-was-I-doing speech was given to me. My parents were so involved in their own problems that they never realized that I was sneaking out and getting involved in things that a twelve-year-old shouldn't be doing. It was too late for me to turn it around by the time this was exposed. I was already too far into drugs to even care what they thought. I was already fighting and had a strong drug habit. I was on my way to following in my biological father's footsteps. The sad thing was, I didn't care.

## *Chapter 9*

# MY OTHER HOME

I started my teenage life—my thirteenth birthday—by spending it in juvenile hall. I ended up with a 45-day sentence for my PCP arrest. I did my time at the Riverside County Juvenile Hall. Because of my age, I ended up in Group 4 within the facility, which was the unit for all the kids who were ages twelve and younger. At the time, the juvenile hall consisted of four dorm-style units for boys, one dorm-style unit for girls, one maximum unit for boys that had single-room cells, and one big unit in the gym for the boys who had been sentenced and were doing Ricardo-M time. Ricardo-M time refers to a short-term commitment to juvenile hall imposed as a condition of probation in a juvenile delinquency case. All the dorm-style units were divided by age, so the higher the group number, the older the guys.

Since this was my first time, I was put in Group 4, and it was a nightmare for me. Not that I didn't like it, but the kids in that unit were so immature. I had been hanging out with older guys, so I was mature for my age. However, these guys were crying all night, acting up like little kids. I would see them go off on the staff and end up being taken down by them, placed in handcuffs, and put in a holding cell. This was a constant scenario. There were about forty of us in that unit, and our ages varied at that time from eight to twelve years old.

Since my mindset was that of a gangster, I carried myself different from the other kids in my unit. It showed too, I never acted up like the others, and I got respect from the other guys in my unit. There were a handful of homies who were about eleven and twelve years old. All seven of us were from different barrios in the county.

I remember one morning waking up and seeing some of the older homies from my barrio in the dorm. My home-boys Thumper and Grumpy were in my unit on a medical visit from Twin Pines, which was a boy's camp in Mount San Jacinto. They remembered me from the barrio, and Thumper called me over. We talked a little bit, and he told me to represent "the Crown" right and not to act up like the little kids. I always remembered that. It was the first advice from one of my homies who was on "the inside"—in prison. After talking with him for about twenty minutes, he was called out for his medical appointment and never returned. He went back up the mountain.

That advice stuck in my head—I was representing my barrio. How I acted and carried myself would reflect on my homies. I didn't want to make us look bad, so I ensured that I carried myself with respect. As my time went on, I began to see more and more of the homies from my barrio. I would watch them to see how they acted, how they carried themselves. Since it was my first time, I wanted to make sure that when I got out, I would have that same respect from my homies, and not be known as a punk.

I liked being there for those 45 days. I adapted very well in there. I had gained a lot of respect. Not just from my homies, but from other homeboys in the other barrios. It was a respect that I enjoyed. Soon it was time for me to go home. My first time in juvie hall was alright. I liked doing the time. I met new homies from different barrios; and my homeboys from my barrio who were there with me were now seeing me on a different respect level. I felt accepted by them, that acceptance created a deep loyalty to my barrio. At thirteen years old, my life was sold out to my barrio. I knew at that time that my life would be to make myself known not just in streets, but in the system. Doing time was easy. It wasn't what I had thought it would be; in fact, it was too easy for me. I knew I would be back.

After doing my time, I went back to school and one of the young homies had hit me up, so we ended up getting into a fight. I beat him up and he called his older brother who was in high school. Word got out quickly and one of the homegirls gave me a heads up that they were coming for me after school. Since these guys were older, I wasn't sure what to expect, so I made a phone call to my one of my uncles who was in a gang.

By the time school ended, the teachers found out that there was going to be some trouble. They took me to the principal's office to protect me. I remember my uncle rolling in deep with a couple of other of his homeboys, to ensure that no one was going to jump me. The other guy's brothers and his friends quickly backed off; however, I was still in the office and the staff wouldn't let me go.

I remember Uncle Gato walking into the office and telling the principle that he was my uncle. He was wearing his gang jacket and had a big knife on him. My uncle was in a local gang, the Scarlets. It was the first time I had seen the school staff afraid, and I loved it. I no longer respected them, I was in awe of their fear as my uncle told them he was taking me, and didn't care if they called the police or not. We walked out of the office and got into a car with a few other homies and we drove off. The next day the other young homie and I talked and squashed our differences.

That first fight was a confidence builder. I had no fear of fighting. It created an adrenaline high for me. I remember my homeboy Rick and I were walking home one day with a few of the other homies who were in the Los Visioneros gang. Rick started to call out a few of the homies to see who wanted to fight him. A couple of them passed so when he asked me. I said, "Let's go." We ended up fighting at the park near our school. Rick and I would fight each other throughout my young life. Even when I got into the Los Visioneros gang, he and I continued to fight. It was an on-going battle between us to fight each other.

I'm sure we both had a lot of respect for one another, because we both knew that neither one of us would back down. Soon after the fighting began, I would pick up my next case (be charged for a new crime committed), and be back in juvie hall.

## Chapter 10

# GET OUT!

I had only been out of juvie hall about a month and half when I came home pretty high on PCP. I don't remember getting home. I found out later that one of my homeboys drove me home. Well, after my mom let me in the house, she called the cops on me because she said she was trying to help me. Little did she know that she wasn't helping me the way she thought. It didn't teach me anything. It just drove me farther away from her and my family. I actually believed that turning me in was her way of sending me off so she wouldn't have to deal with me. She was still dealing with Dad's infidelity, and whenever I was there it added fuel to their fight. It felt that she was setting me aside for him. However, it didn't matter by this time because I was too set in my ways to change. It didn't matter what she said, I had a mission in life. I was set to fulfill my revenge.

After doing my time, I got out and was approached by my homeboy Spider. He had let me know that they were getting some homies together and starting a new clicka (street gang) together. He asked if I wanted in, and they wanted me to go to the first meeting in the barrio. It was on a Friday night when all active gangs in Corona had their meetings at the barrio. So there we were starting our new gang. The first day in the gang I got into a fight with one of the other local gang (Los Visioneros) members. Yup, you guessed it—Rick. He had come over with his gang asking what we were doing and who gave us permission to start a new gang in the hood? He called a couple of the guys out, and when he came to me, since I had already fought him in the past, I jumped up and we walked down the alley and fought.

There wasn't a day that passed that I didn't get into a fight. I was getting into so many fights every day that my knuckles were always cut up. It was obvious from the start of this new gang, I was doing most of the fighting. I didn't care, though, I had motives that no one knew about but me.

I would get caught for being under the influence of PCP and was booked on many assault charges throughout my teenage life. I was in juvenile hall more than I was out. Every time I was let out of juvie, I would be back in within a month or so. I became well known on the inside, not just by those in the hall with me, but also by the staff. Most of the time they referenced the guys by their last name, but I was on a first name basis, because they knew me that well. I remember a couple of the staff would tell me that if I kept up my current lifestyle, I would end up in prison in no time—or end up dead. They saw no future in me, I was a reckless young man with no hope.

My life was really spiraling out of control. I had a bad temper. I recall one day when I heard my mom and dad fighting in their room. I had a gun on me, I waited for my dad to come out so I could shoot him. I wanted to kill him. I had so much hate for him and no respect for him at all. I began to think of all the things I went through, and my heart filled with rage. I paced the hallway a couple of times waiting for him to come out. I was going to take him out.

As I paced, my little sister Christina came up to me and asked me if I was okay. She was maybe three or four years old. I looked at her and thought about how I felt when my biological dad was killed—the pain of it hit me, and I couldn't let my little sister or brothers go through that. But I was still so mad that I walked outside to cool off. I couldn't be there in that house. I didn't trust myself. I knew at that moment that I couldn't be at the house when he was there. I wanted to kill him. I couldn't trust myself to be in the same place with him so I hung out on the streets a lot, just so I wouldn't be at home. If I wasn't partying with the homies, I was doing time. One thing was certain, I couldn't be home.

Some time passed and dad moved out. It didn't matter to me, I was still partying and my gang was really my new family now. Throughout all this craziness, I would hear the voice of the Lord sometimes call my name. There had been a few times when I would feel the Holy Spirit speak to me audibly, especially when my life was threatened. Whenever something really bad happened, I would hear the voice of the Lord tell me to leave. It was strange to me to know that in the middle of all my craziness, He was watching over me.

I recall a time when I was walking home and I began to feel the presence of God on my life. It was a strong, heavy presence. It is hard to explain the heaviness, but I knew it was the Lord. I began to feel convicted of the way I was living. Something happened on that walk home. By the time I got home, I told my mom to call her pastor because I needed prayer.

The pastor arrived and we prayed. I asked the Lord into my life. After we prayed, the pastor asked me what was I going to tell my friends. Then he asked the million-dollar question, what was I going to do about my gang? I sat there for a minute and said that I was going to get out. He asked me what would that look like. I wasn't sure, but I knew that the worst-case scenario was that I would have to walk the line. Walking the line was when the gang members lined up in two parallel lines and I would walk through the middle, as they beat me.

I made a few calls to my gang members and announced that I was getting out because I wanted to go to church. Most of them were shocked, since I was the one always in the mix. I was told I would have to come to the meeting and fight my way out. This was on a Wednesday that I made that decision, so I had till Friday to pray and seek the Lord for strength.

Friday night rolled up on me and I went to the barrio for the meeting. We started the meeting as normal as other gangs were having their meetings. First order of business was me. They VP of the gang asked me, "So what's up Travieso, you getting out ese?" I responded, "Yea, I am. What do I need to do?" He responded, "Tu sabes, you need to walk the line ese, it doesn't matter if you're going to church."

As I looked around the circle. I noticed some of them didn't want to look at me. I wasn't fearful of them, I just wanted them to feel the amazing peace I had in my heart. I waited as they all began to line up. Someone said, "Whenever you're ready." As I walked toward the lines, I said a little silent prayer and then stepped into the middle of the two lines of gangsters. I remember feeling them hit me, their fists crunching against my body and head.

After it was all said and done, a couple of them shook my hand, and asked me if I was okay. I said, "Yes, I'm good." I left the meeting and went to Uncle Popeye and Tia Rosie's house. They lived around the corner from the barrio. I went there to check the damages to my face. I had felt like nothing happened to me. As I walked in, Aunt Rosie asked me if I got out of the gang. I told her I did. She said, "Oh, you didn't have to fight?" I told her I did. She said, "By the looks of you, I can't even tell you were fighting." I went to the bathroom and looked in the mirror—sure enough, nothing was wrong with my face. I couldn't see a scratch or bruise anywhere. I believe the Lord had His hand upon me.

Within the next couple of weeks, I was bringing young homies to church with me. God was moving in me and using me to bring my homeboys to Christ. I began to hang out with the homies more so I could bring them in. Rather than changing them, I ended up backsliding and getting back into the old gang ways. I think my church episode only lasted for about two months. Next thing I knew, I was back on the streets and up to no good. I was charged again and back to juvie I went.

## Chapter 11

# BACK AT IT

I had been going in and out of juvie and boys' homes as a result of my drug abuse and fighting. Over the course of a couple of years, I had been to two boys' homes and AWOL out of the juvenile hall. After some time had passed, I had accumulated several pages of charges against me and the judge considered having me go to the California Youth Authority. My mom came up with an idea for me to go to live with Aunt Martha and Uncle Manuel in San Diego, California. Her brother (my Uncle Jessie) did that when he was younger, and it helped him as a young man, so my mom thought it might help me, too. The judge went for it, but he placed some conditions including that I couldn't return to the county of Riverside until I was eighteen years old. At the time of sentencing, I was fourteen just shy of my fifteenth birthday.

Living in San Diego didn't really help me as much as my mother had wanted. I developed a heroin addiction, which led me to more drug connections. My cousin Junior was from a local barrio in San Diego and he began introducing me to his homies. I hit it off with all of them. They started coming by to pick me up to hang out with them. My life never changed for the better; it only seemed to get worse. Since I really didn't want change, it didn't matter where I went or lived—I was always in the middle of chaos.

As a matter of fact, I ended up getting arrested and being sent to the San Diego County Juvenile Hall for drugs and fighting with some guys from the San Diego barrios. When I got to juvie hall, I went in gangbanging, representing my barrio. I was all by myself, since I was the only one from River-side county, and they slammed me down until I went to court and saw the judge the second time. By the second time, the court now had my rap sheet and turned me over to Riverside County Probation. I knew I was going away for some time.

I ended up going to another boys' home in Ontario. For some reason the judge didn't send me to the Youth Author-ity. While I was going to court and then waiting for place-ment to pick me up, I was in Unit 2 with my homeboy Pelon. He was the president of the Visioneros gang in my barrio. We really hit it off and became really close to one another. In the streets I was always fighting with his gang members, but now being locked up with him, he told me he wanted me in his gang. He said he would tell his members who were there in the juvie hall with us. Word quickly got out that I was getting in. It was a wrap. I was now a Visionero. Some of the homies in the Visioneros were not too sure about me, because they still had issues with me, but all that was over. I now was one of them.

I went to placement, and after a couple of months I was out on a weekend furlough. The first thing I did was meet up with my new gang members. We had talked about some of the issues we had and took care of our issues. After we dealt with them, there I was back in the mix again. It wasn't long before I was kicked out of the placement home and was sent to Twin Pines Ranch. I really enjoyed being at the ranch because there were homies there from Riverside and San Bernardino counties. All of us were between sixteen and eighteen years old, and all the homies were very active in their gangs. The ranch wasn't like juvie hall or any other placement. The homies there were more mature and more street smart. We were the A-team of our local gangs so to speak.

When the time came for me to graduate from the program, I had done a total of two years and nine months. Because I was incarcerated, I never attended public high school; I missed out on my high school days. I was released from Twin Pines on May 5, 1988. I was excited, I knew there was a month left of school, so I thought I would get to experience high school for the last month, but my probation officer (PO) said, "Don't even think about it, Hernandez. If I hear that you're anywhere near that high school, I am violating your probation." I wasn't wanted in the schools. I had caused so much trouble when I was in junior high that the school officials had told my PO that I couldn't be on school property.

So there I was, a seventeen-year-old with a lot of time on my hands. Things had changed so much in the time that I was gone. Our barrio wasn't the same. A lot of my homeboys were even dressing different. I was still stuck in my khaki pants, Pendleton shirts, and gang jacket. I stuck out like a sore thumb. I wanted things to be the way they used to be. I had to find out where everyone was now that things had changed.

I remember one night my homeboy Rebel and I were at a party. We were selling some acid (LSD), and we met up with this girl named Brenda, who later became my wife. She was selling PCP and we traded some acid for some PCP. She was pretty. What caught my eye was that she was dressed old-school. She wasn't into the new style. Rebel and I left the party and I asked him about the girl. He kind of laughed and said, "Homie, forget about it, you don't have chance."

After about a couple of months had passed, my home-boy Junior and I were cruising and he asked me if I wanted to go to his prima's (girl cousin) place. He said that a lot of the homies hang out there. We went and I found out that his cousin's roommate was Brenda, the girl from the party. I didn't say too much, but I kept my eyes on her, watching how she carried herself. I liked everything about her. She was old-school and knew what was going on. At first, she didn't like me at all. I don't even know if she remembered who I was. In fact, she didn't care at all for the Visioneros, since her brother and cousins were in our rival gang, the Demonios.

She wasn't into me at all, but I was never attracted to anyone like I was to her—this girl was different. Something I never knew existed in me came alive. I was set on getting to know who his girl was.

# Chapter 12

# I'm in Love

It didn't take long to develop a friendship with this beautiful girl named Brenda Fredericks. We discovered that we had a lot in common, and we became best friends in a matter of weeks. It was like the Lord accelerated our friendship. We became inseparable. Deep down I wanted to be more than friends, but I had a few issues that needed to be resolved.

I began to realize that if I was going to make this work, then I would have to kick my existing addictions. I had started to use heroin, and it wasn't that bad yet, so I went home and kicked the drug cold turkey. It took about a week and half to go through the withdraws of it. Since Brenda had two beautiful little girls, ages four and two, I knew I would have to change my life if I had a chance with her.

I didn't tell her I was using heroin; she only thought I was using speed (methamphetamine). So when I suddenly disappeared without saying a word to anyone to go home to kick my drug habit, she was a little upset with me. My mother didn't seem to care for Brenda, so when she came looking for me, she was told I wasn't home.

Then one day I show up seemingly out of nowhere and, of course, Brenda gave me the third degree, wondering where I was. I told her about my drug use and that I was clean from the heroin. However, we both continued to use meth. I ended up satisfying my urge to shoot heroin by shooting up speed. I was still pretty messed up.

One morning after I had spent the night with Brenda, one of my gang members, who had just been released from jail, came to our place and hit me up for some issues he had with me. He and I went outside in the alley and got into a fight. I was so mad at him and my gang that I told him I was out of the gang. I was done with their madness. He said that it wasn't going to be that easy because there was some unfinished business. The homies came to Brenda's place looking for me because the unfinished business was a personal matter. I let them know that I didn't need them to handle it for me, that I would do it myself. But my gang wouldn't let up. They were torn between the two of us, me and my other homeboy who got in a fight. Eventually they let me go. Don't get me wrong, there were some things that went down that I can't write about, but let's just say that the Lord saw me through all that craziness.

Shortly afterward, my mom informed me that my dad was moving back in with her, that she was going to give him another chance. That was my cue to move out. With Brenda and I developing our relationship, she said I could move in with her. At the time I was also real close to my homeboy Rebel. He was living in Riverside with his girlfriend Reggie, and they both said I could live with them since Rebel had been staying with me for some time at my mom's house.

If it hadn't been for Brenda assuring me that it was okay for me to stay with her, my life may have taken a different turn. I look back at that crucial choice I made that placed me where I am now. The Lord had it all worked out for my life. Even then in the midst of my craziness, the Lord had His hand over me.

I told Brenda that I was moving in with her. I went home, packed what little clothes I had there, and that was that. I now was moved out of my parents' home—yet I was still only seventeen years old. I let my probation officer know the circumstances and he was okay with me making the move. There was nothing my mom could do; she was really upset that I moved out. However, she knew that she had no control over me whatsoever. Little did she know at the time that this was the best thing for me.

Now, here we are—Brenda, her daughters, Andrea and Jeanette, and me in a room that she had been renting. I was a little scared of the situation because now life became so much more than me. I now had the responsibility of this little family. I will share one story that I will always remember as Brenda and I started our life together. We had a little talk with Andrea and Jeanette about me joining the family. Andrea had asked in this conversation what she should call me. We let her know that it was her decision. With that said, we were at a Kmart shopping store later that week, and all of sudden I hear Andrea calling out for me as loud as she could, "STEPFATHER, STEPFATHER, can you buy this for me?" I was really embarrassed. I was only seventeen years old, and this four-year-old was calling me her stepfather, it reminded me of a wicked old man. We chuckle over it now.

After moving in, Brenda and I quickly fell in love with each other. I proposed to her and she said yes. Because we didn't have any money to get married, we decided to try to save some so we could have a wedding. It was really difficult to save because we both had an expensive meth addiction. Like previously mentioned, I began shooting up speed to replace the heroin urge. I think it was the use of a needle that I was hooked on, because the high was instant.

Thankfully, though, our lives would change for the better. The Lord was doing something even in the midst of our drug use and wild living.

# Chapter 13

# CHANGE IS COMING

Things in our lives began to change, Brenda and I had been living together for about two and half years when she told me she was pregnant with our first child our son, Frank Jr. I remember when he was born—I was so proud. I can recall the first time the nurse put him in my arms. I wanted to shout and cry all at the same time. This was my boy. Deep down I wanted to do the right thing, but we were still in our lifestyle of drug addiction. Deep down inside of me, there was something calling out for change. This reminds me of one of the things that the Lord has shown me since then— everyone knows what's wrong with them, but there aren't too many who know what's right with them. That was me. I didn't know what was right with me. I was disappointed with myself, so I covered it up with more drugs, because that was all I knew.

My life was a mess, and I was dragging my family through the mud of shame and despair. I had been working at a good paying job; however due to our drug addiction, all the money was being blown on the drugs. The job only enabled me to have more drugs. A job wasn't the problem; the problem was me. Brenda and I were constantly fighting. I became the one thing I despised most, an abusive person toward her. Since I had witnessed abuse growing up, I didn't want to be that person, but here I was making the same mistakes. I hated myself. I couldn't even look at myself in the mirror. I knew I needed to change.

Brenda talked to me about going to church. I didn't want to talk about it and would change the subject. Deep down I knew she was right. I eventually gave in to her. I remember one story that really shook me. We were living in an apartment and my grandmother had come to stay with us because Brenda wanted her with us, so she could pray for us. Grandma was a strong woman of faith. I was still shooting up meth. I couldn't kick the habit. Brenda had told my grandmother everything, she admitted to her how addicted we were.

One time, in the middle of the night, Brenda and Grandma said that I jumped up like a cat, my body was bent, and I started to growl and claw at Brenda. My grandmother jumped up too and started to pray and cast the demon out of me. I turned back around, got into bed, and went to sleep. The next morning, I was by myself. Brenda and my grandma were in the kitchen praying for me. We all slept in the front room, so I wasn't necessarily by myself. As I woke up, they told me the story of how I had attacked Brenda and how I was growling. I don't remember a thing. I knew then that I needed Jesus. I wanted change, and this was the last straw.

Soon thereafter Brenda became pregnant with our second son, Albert. I didn't want any more children, so this news took me by surprise. Brenda and I had just started a new life. We started fresh. One night while we were in bed, she mentioned that she was being convicted by the Holy Spirit to get married, or else I would have to move back with my mother. We both knew that wasn't an option. I had wanted to give Brenda a big wedding, so that was why we hadn't got married. But now, we both agreed to get married. She planned the whole thing in a week and we were married on Christmas Eve in 1992. It was a very small ceremony, nothing fancy. To this day, I wish I could've done more, but we got married and I'm proud to have her as my wife.

On July 6, 1993, Albert was born. We were all so happy. Our daughters were a little older and Frank Jr. was four years old. Brenda and I were both sober and serving the Lord. Even though we weren't on drugs and serving the Lord, there was something inside of me making a demand on the call on my life. At the time, I really didn't know what it was. I seemed to have everything together. I had my marriage, my children, a job. We were doing good, but deep down there was a tugging in my heart. I wouldn't know what that was until years later, as I began to see God's specific call on my life.

Brenda and I both had a deep desire to serve Jesus. Whatever it entailed; we were up for the challenge. We got married in a little church called Church of Praise. It was a great church. We were excited to be part of this church family. The problem was, though, we just were going through the motions of Christianity. We really didn't understand that our walk with Jesus was a relationship—not a religion.

After a year or so had passed, we backslid and ended up on the drugs again, but thankfully that lasted only a short time. This time I returned to the Lord first. I went back to the church where I first met the Lord as a young boy, Goodnews Church. It was a big church that was in the middle of a revival. They were having a service every day for about two years. Brenda wasn't ready to return to church, so I would go by myself. Sometimes I would take little Frank with me—just my son and I going to service. Pastor Kurt Schroeder was the senior pastor and he took a liking to me right away. I was impressed that he knew me by my first name and was looking out for me.

Eventually Brenda came to church with me and we picked up where we left off in our Christian walk with the Lord. Pastor Kurt had a brother in the church disciple me. His name was Richard. He would play a significant role in my life in this season. He began to mentor and disciple me. Also at that time there was another brother who was from my barrio who kept in touch with me, Orencio Rubio. He had met me when I was about thirteen years old. Orencio had attended a church with my mom, and always looked out for me. As I got older, he would keep tabs on me and would show up on my doorstep when I was fighting with my wife or going through a bad time. He would knock on my door, always with a bag of groceries, and say I was on his mind. He wanted to bless me. He always had a big smile on his face. He and Richard helped me and poured the love of Jesus into my life as a young Christian.

## Chapter 14

# HERE WE GO AGAIN

Goodnews Church moved to Riverside, and out of that church came Presence of the Lord Church led by Pastor Steve Gonzales and Pastor Manuel Perez. We attended that church for about five years since it was closer to where we lived in Corona. We worked with the youth, Sunday School children, and were also the custodians, along with another couple.

As the fifth year rolled in at Presence of the Lord Church, I had a second job. Throughout those five years I had been working as a security guard at the local mall, and my second job was with the school district, also as a security guard, at a local high school. What I thought was a blessing, was actually a stumbling block. I worked so many hours that we stopped attending church; we stopped fellowshipping with our church family. Most of all, our relationship with Jesus took a back seat. Soon everything started crashing around us. My father-in-law, aunt, and my little brother Angel died within a month of one another. With all that taking place, I went deep again into the world of gangs and drugs. I began to hang out with the younger generation of homies from my barrio. This setback was different. It wasn't just the drugs I now was exposing my family to—but also gang life.

The homies I was hanging out with were causing a lot of chaos in the neighborhood. I was going to street rumbles, and soon I was carrying guns again because of the enemies I was creating in the streets. I was in the middle of all the craziness that the gang life had to offer. I was so involved that I didn't even realize what I was doing anymore. I was carrying a gun everywhere I went. I no longer trusted anyone. The homies I was hanging out with were a different breed. This new generation no longer valued life. It was shoot first, ask questions later. It was a dog-eat-dog world, and I was in the midst of some crazy stuff.

I recall one incident. I was in the middle of a deal where I would be coming into some money. One of the youngsters was going through some hard times, so I volunteered to help him out. My mom and his mom were best friends when they were younger, so I knew him for a long time. While my deal had not gone through yet, this homie shows up at my doorstep, and pulls a gun on me, telling me he wasn't leaving my house until I gave him something he could sell. He had already been doing some bad things in the hood, so I knew he would shoot if I didn't produce something. I was furious! I had never been robbed, so my pride got the best of me. Of all days, I wasn't carrying a gun. So, I gave him a laptop.

Soon after, a couple of my homies and I were planning on getting him. Just before we were ready to leave to gun him down, I heard the Lord's voice saying, "What are you doing?" Then He showed me the guy's mother. I couldn't do it. I grew a conscience and decided to pull back. Everything eventually worked out. One of the older homies talked with the guy who robbed me and it was all resolved. I knew the Lord was keeping me, even though my mind was telling me to do something different.

It wouldn't be long after that when our house was raided by the Irvine Police Department (PD). I was taken in as well as my daughter Andrea. They eventually let her go and kept me. I got bailed out of the Orange County Jail. However, that didn't slow me down. The district attorney (DA) for Orange County didn't pick up the case; it was turned over to Riverside County DA for some unknown reason. Usually the DA of the county the crime was committed in, is the one that will prosecute the case. In this case the DA of Orange County decided to not pursue the case, so Riverside County picked up the case to charge me with. So I was picked up at my house once again on a felony warrant. This time it was me and my wife. I didn't understand how that went down. I had been out for about six months. Now Corona PD is hooking me and my wife up. We both got bailed out shortly thereafter. I had felt that the Corona Police were gunning for me and my wife, I had to think fast. I couldn't let my wife do time. She needed to be out with our kids.

Our court papers made us out to be some crazy villains, so I began to think if I could talk to the DA, I could help our case.

Our public defenders were jokes. They didn't care what happened to us. They were talking eight years in prison for my crime, and two years for my wife, so I followed through with this crazy idea I thought of in the court room. As one of my court proceedings finished, I followed the DA assigned to my case into the elevator. I was with my wife and mother. I told him, "Look, what you see on paper, isn't me. I mean yes, I committed the crime, but I haven't always been a criminal." I told him that I had a worked at the local mall and knew several police officers from working there. If he would ask them about me, I was sure they would say some nice things about me. I needed him to know that what was on paper wasn't always my life. There was a short time when I was doing well; working at the mall allowed me to develop friendships with some police officers when I worked as a security guard there.

On my next court date, the DA approached me and said, "Okay, I asked a couple of the officers, and they spoke highly of you. What happened?" I didn't go into any details, just that I had made some bad choices. He asked what was I expecting from him. I said, "Give me whatever you want, I just don't want my wife doing time." So he suspended her sentence with three years' probation, and I was sentenced to a year in the county jail, and was released on a work release program two months later.

I was supposed to work on the Cal-Trans (freeway crew). That didn't last and I soon picked up another case, (was charged with another new crime) and was on the run. I managed to stay out for about a year running and living in the motels with my wife. We were both strung out on drugs and still hanging out with the homies. Our kids were living with both our parents. I really didn't seem to care, since I knew I couldn't take care of them. I was too involved in what I wanted. My wife was asking me to stop, but I was too mixed up to pay any attention to her.

One night around 1 a.m., we had just returned to our motel room after hanging out with a couple of the homies. Next door there was a gas station with a market inside. I told Brenda that I would be back, I was going to the store. As I was walking back to our room, I heard someone say, "Frank, wait up." I couldn't see who it was, but as the voice came closer, I saw it was a police officer. I was stuck. I couldn't run. I was cornered. "Who you talking to?" I asked.

He said, "You're Frank Hernandez, right?"

"No, I'm not." I had a fake ID on me so I tried to play it off. I almost got away with it. But I ended up in the back of the police car. It was a wrap.

Now I was back in court for my arraignment hearing. Everything that I was running from was now in my face. I told my wife and mom not to even come to court because I knew I was going to have to face up to the things I was running from. My wife believed that everything was going to be okay. Deep down, I knew it wasn't. There was my previous charge, and now there was the additional new charges I was facing.

The same DA from my first court proceedings walked in and said, "No more running, no more games. I am giving you five years. If you don't sign for it now, I am going after your wife and you. Either sign now or I will pick her up tonight, your choice." I said, "Where do I sign?" I signed and was given five years in prison.

# *Chapter 15*

# PRISON TIME

It was still dark outside as the sheriff's correctional officer called out my name. It was my time to leave the county jail and catch my ride to the prison yard. I was taken to a holding cell labeled Southern Hispanics. I noticed other holding cells labels indicating Whites, Blacks, and others. As I approached the officer, he went through my property to separate what I could take with me and what I had to either throw away or mail home. Soon after that, I was given a paper jumpsuit, handcuffed, and shackled to be taken to Kern Valley State Prison in Delano, California.

As I boarded the green sheriff bus, I noticed a guard to the rear of the bus holding a mini-14 rifle. I was only used to a county bus ride—this ride was different. This bus had murderers, kidnappers, gangbangers, and every criminal you could think of. There was even a small cage inside the bus that held the protective custody inmates. This was now the real thing, there was no turning back. I had heard so many stories of prison, now I was about to experience life on the prison yard.

As we arrived in Delano, I saw the big fence with razor-sharp wires and the electrical shock warning signs on the second set of fencing around the whole prison. I was taking it all in, as everyone was talking and some were even excited about going back to the prison yard. They were saying that doing state time was so much better than county time. I soon would agree with them.

As we drove into the sally port, we were met by several correctional officers. We were moved into a big room where we were again separated by our ethnicity and by our gang affiliation. It was a little shocking to me that the correctional officers were okay with the gang lifestyle inside the prison; it appeared they approved of it. They were fully aware of the way the different gangs operated inside the prison yard. Once inside, they lined us all up and stripped-searched us. There was no privacy whatsoever. As prior inmates, we were used to that, having no privacy. So the long process of intake began.

As we were being taken to our unit, a correctional sergeant stood on a table just outside our unit prior to us entering. It was just us Southern Hispanics who were left to enter; the whites, blacks, Northern Hispanics, and others had already entered their units. The sergeant told us that this unit was just cleared from being a protective custody (PC) unit. So, we would be given a few minutes to write a letter to the homies in the other yards notifying them we were not a PC unit any more. I was shocked that they knew what was up. Then a homie from East LA took roll call on who we were and what barrios we represented. Then the word was given that our unit was no longer a PC unit but a general population yard. At that, my time in prison began.

After a few months in the reception yard at Delano, I had no contact from the outside, there were no letters, no phone calls, nothing. This was the normal procedure for your first 90 days or so in prison reception. I was getting involved in some dumb things on the yard. I figured this is prison, it's survival here, I'm going to have to prove myself. Things around me were not too good. It was a wake-up call for me. As my fourth month in prison was coming up, I got word that I would be going to Susanville to finish my time. Susanville was a prison in Northern California that prepared inmates for Fire Camp. Fire Camp is a program in California where inmates are trained to help fight wild fires or clear forests and freeways in exchange for time off, extra custody credits, better food, etc.

I was shackled with one of my homeboys, Dennis, on the long twelve-hour bus ride to Susanville. We had known one another for a long time in the barrio. So, we talked a lot about our families and about some of the things going on in our barrio. It was a long, grueling ride, but riding up with my homeboy Dennis made it a little more tolerable. One thing I recall is that they served us lots of peanut butter sandwiches. When asked why, I was told so that we wouldn't have to use the restroom. There was no way to use it when shackled up and wearing a paper jumpsuit.

After we arrived at Susanville, Dennis and I were hit up by one of the inmate clerks who was a homie from another barrio. He asked us where were we from. We told him Corona. He said that there were a lot of our homies in the yard. He went to the office, looked us up, and let us know what yards we were going to. Dennis and I went to two different yards. It was evening when we separated and prepared to enter our new prison yard.

While waiting by the gate to the prison yard, a couple of homies from El Monte hit me up and asked me where was I from. I told them I was from Corona, shook their hands, and introduced myself. They said they would let my homies know I was coming in. It took about an hour for me to progress through. As I entered the yard, there were some inmates in the yard, as it was evening yard time. The yard was big and surrounded by two-story brick dormitories. There were a couple of handball courts and some various chin and pull-up bars. I could see the segregation of the various prison gangs in the yard.

I went up to my dorm, and as I entered, I was shown where my bunk was. A couple of the homies in my dorm told me I had some love from my homeboys. As I looked at my bunk, I saw some new sweats, shoes, some coffee, and a can of tobacco. My homie Adolph had hooked me up. I started to unpack and get comfortable in my new house, so to speak. I looked over my shoulder and there was Adolph with a big grin. He gave me a big hug as we hadn't seen one another for several years. He helped me unpack and gave me a rundown on who was on the yard from our barrio.

He let me in on the yard issues so I knew what to expect. It was a couple of hours that we sat and talked. Then he introduced me to the homies in the dorm. The dorm housed twenty guys. There were about eight homies and the rest were white and black guys.

The next morning, we went to the yard. My homeboy Mosca had told me that he was going to prepare me for Fire Camp training, which consisted of one to two weeks of intense physical training. Since I was out of shape, it took me actually two weeks to pass the physical training. I didn't get into the training right away. My homie Mosca ran a mile with me every day, which helped prepare me for the training. If he hadn't gone out of his way to push me to run, I may not have gone to Fire Camp and would have been stuck on the yard.

I remember when I first got to Susanville, I was in line to see my counselor. One of the homies from my dorm who was from Long Beach (Longo) said he would go with me because he too needed to see his counselor. As we waited in line, we were sitting on a bench and he told me that something was about to kick-off, but it wasn't our fight. Just sit and watch, he said. He motioned over to the Northern Hispanics workout area. There was an older guy maybe in his early 40s doing some pull-ups, and three young guys went up to him and stabbed him with some makeshift prison knives made from toothbrushes and razor blades. The sirens went off and the yard was shut down. The correctional officers came and took away the three young guys and an ambulance came and picked up the older guy. We all returned to our normal day. I was stunned—like wow, no investigation, no nothing. It hit me. I was seeing what I had thought prison to be. There was nowhere to run, this was it.

On my first weekend and for just about every weekend thereafter, Brenda drove all the way from home to prison to see me. She was working two jobs and then on the weekend making the long fifteen-hour drive to see me. It was crazy of her to drive week after week to see me, but there was no stopping her. Don't get me wrong, I enjoyed her coming up and getting to see her and my children, but I worried about her and the drive, especially during the winter when it would rain and snow. Those visits allowed us to draw strength from one another.

As I got closer to going to Fire Camp, I remember that the Lord had been dealing with me. I began to hear Him speak to me so clearly. I knew it was Him, yet I wasn't ready to turn my life over. I thought that if I kept doing wrong things, I would chase His presence away. One day in our dorm, we were all watching a high-speed chase, and, of course, we were rooting for the driver to get away.

Then the Holy Spirit spoke audibly to me. He said "Frank, that is you running." I paid no attention to Him. Again He spoke the same thing. I didn't say anything, but it was like He knew what I was thinking. I had thought, "What do You mean that's me?" He said, "You are running from Me. You can either surrender and serve Me, or you will crash and serve Me. It's your choice—but I have called you to serve Me."

I got angry and began to cuss out loud and said, "Turn that stupid show off." Everyone just looked at me like I was weird. No one knew what was going on inside me.

The following weekend after a visit with Brenda, one of the older homies asked me to walk a couple of laps around the yard with him. He wanted to talk with me. During our walk, he said, "Frank, who else gets visits here on the yard? What homies get the love that you get week after week?" I said, "No one, why?" I thought, "Here it comes, he's going to ask me to bring something in."

He said, "Think about that." Then after a few moments of silence, he said, "I had what you had. I had a good woman who was there for me like your wife. Think about what you got, homie, you're different. All the homies aren't like you, you're a natural. You have two choices. You can choose the homies and your wife may wait for you if you come back, two maybe three times. But eventually she will get tired and you will lose what you got. Or you can stop the craziness and keep what you got. You're older already, you don't have nothing to prove, homie. I know you read your Bible every now and then, if that is what you want, don't be afraid to make that stand. If I could help change one man's life, after I destroyed mine, I will be happy."

I was shocked and was left standing with my thoughts—I knew that this advice was God-sent. Soon afterward I would be on my way to Fire Camp.

## Chapter 16

# FIRE CAMP PASTOR

I arrived at the prison Fire Camp in the Trinity River mountains. As we traveled up Highway 299, the scenery was beautiful. We traveled passed Trinity River and a small community, Weaverville, which reminded me of a Western movie. When I got off the bus at the camp, I met up with a couple of the homies from the prison yard, as well as one of my homies from my neighborhood. The camp was a big change from the yard—it was so much better, more laid back, and more things to do to help make our time pass by without all the craziness of the prison yard.

Soon afterward, my homeboy Clumsy arrived at the Fire Camp. He and I became close, as we both were on the same fire crew and were from the same barrio. We watched over one another. One day after work, we came back to the camp and the homies were telling us that the sergeant of the camp was removing Clumsy and I from the camp and taking us to a different camp. I'm not sure why we were removed, but when he drove us to our new camp, he just said that we were no longer welcomed at his camp.

This new camp was nothing like our first one; it was run-down, in the boonies, no nice view, no nice dorms. It was an older camp, and the buildings were old, too, and in need of work. One thing it did have that no other camp had was a chapel. Since I had started to really follow the Lord in my previous camp, it was nice to have a chapel. I immediately got hooked up in the chapel and met the other guys who were serving the Lord there. The following Saturday I met the prison pastors, Ron and Debra Freise. These two would become mentors in my life as I served out my prison time in this camp.

As time progressed at the camp, my homeboy Clumsy and I would get to be good friends, which allowed me to minister to him. I knew he didn't know too much about the Lord, so I mentored him as much as I could. I remember one morning Pastor Ron and Debra pulled me aside and told me that God was going to use me in this camp. A few months later, I became the camp pastor, which meant I would be leading Bible studies and helping with the Sunday morning services. I began to use this time as a training ground to build my faith. I knew that once I was released, I would be put in predicaments where I would need to trust the Lord.

As I began to pastor at this camp, the homies began to recognize the faith I had. They had a lot of respect for what I was doing. This place was real laid back with no prison politics from the yard. Don't get me wrong, there were the prison yard rules we all went by, but since this was camp, everyone was a little more laid back and showed respect toward one another. There was a peace that rested over the camp. Even the prison staff were Christians. So, I'm sure that a lot of prayer covered this place.

With Pastor Ron and Debra mentoring me, they showed me how to love my wife. I was witnessing their love for one another, and it began to put a desire in me to love my wife as Ron displayed his love for his wife. His lifestyle was a great example for me to witness.

I soon began to lead the camp Bible study and lead the Sunday morning services. It was evident to the guys in the camp that I was taking my walk seriously. I was hearing the Lord speak to me so clearly in this place. He began to tell me that this is where I would learn to develop faith in Him. I couldn't be there for my family when they were going through life issues, so I was being taught that through my prayers and seeking God, He would see my family through the difficult times.

My faith was being built as my time was coming up for me to go home. I had been praying and the Lord had impressed upon my heart to ask the prison staff if I could come off the fire crew and become a porter in the prison camp. This meant I wouldn't be leaving to fight fires, I would be staying at the camp for the last few months of my prison sentence. The lieutenant of the Fire Camp asked why I wanted to be taken off the fire line, and I told him

I wanted to prepare mentally to go home. Being a porter meant that I would clean the restrooms, showers, and even clean the chapel since there was no porter for our church. They went for it. So, I spent the last four months in camp. While the rest of the inmates were out working in the community doing clean up, I remained in the camp cleaning the restrooms and chapel. This was my alone time to seek the Lord and pray and prepare for my parole date.

January 6, 2006, was the date of my parole. It came fast. I remember the day I left the camp. The homies called me to the side right after breakfast. They all shook my hand and said they were proud of me. They said something to me that caught me by surprise. One of the homies from Pomona said, "Pancho (Spanish name for Frank), we hope you don't come back, homie. We gave you a pass that most people don't get. This is just camp, homeboy. Coming back to prison will not be good next time. Don't make a fool out of us. You go out there and stay serving the Lord."

I told them that there was no turning back for me. I was done with the gang life. He gave me a hug and said to please keep him in my prayers. He said that he wished he could turn his life around like I did, but he was too much in the mix to change now.

I told him, "Homie, it's never too late." I would continue to pray for him. That would be the last time I would see him and the others after I was released from prison.

## *Chapter 17*

# I'M HOME

My wife and mother came to the prison to pick me up so I wouldn't have to take the bus home. It was a cold morning and we were expecting snow. My name was called over the loudspeaker to come to the front office for my release. All the camp came out to see me leave. I had gained a lot of respect from the inmates at the camp. Not just from my homies, but even the other races knew my passion for Jesus. I never held back to pray for them when they needed it. This prison camp really helped me to stay focused on my walk with the Lord.

As I was leaving with my wife and mom, the prison staff in the office said they knew I wouldn't be coming back. They had never seen someone like me. I didn't know what they were talking about. I just was serving the Lord as He led me. Apparently, my turnaround was contagious. One of the staff said, "Frank, this camp will not be the same without you, you really led these men like a real pastor." Those words meant a lot to me. I wasn't trying to stand out or put myself out there like that. I was just being the man the Lord was making me to be—a pastor to broken and wounded people.

Soon we were on our way. I sat in the back seat and I noticed it began to snow. I didn't tell my wife or mom what the Lord was saying to me. He told me that when I arrived in prison, my path was dark and shameful. Now He had cleansed me white as snow. I was literally seeing it as it snowed.

My life was changed, and I knew it. I no longer wanted the things that brought me into the prison system. Now I was free! I knew in my heart that I was a changed man. I could feel the power of the Holy Spirit deep inside me.

It took about twelve hours to drive home. When we arrived home, I was greeted by my two daughters, Andrea and Jeanette, as well as my two sons, Frank Jr. and Albert. I had noticed that Frank Jr. was already following in my old steps. He had the look that I knew all too well. I didn't say anything to him at the time; I didn't want to start up on him since I just got home, but it was in my heart to talk with him.

Several days had passed, and I tried to talk to my son. It was difficult because I hadn't been a father to him—he had literally grown up while I was using drugs and partying with my homies. Then I went to prison. So, he had been influenced by the homies in the barrio. It was a hard lesson learned.

Now I wanted to be a father, but he had no respect for me. He had learned how to survive as a young gangster in the barrio. In my attempt to talk with him, he just blew me off and paid no mind to what I was saying. It had hurt me, but I knew it was my fault. Now I had to earn his respect, since I had pushed him aside for my own selfish desires.

The hard fight for my son was tough. And I would soon be fighting for my daughters and younger son as well. Things had certainly changed in the Hernandez family. No longer were my kids young. I had spent too many years running the streets and my children had grown up without me. Now that my mind was clear, I had no more addictions, and I was ready to be a father, my children had already learned how to live without my input in their life. It was hard for me to face because their choices were not good choices. I didn't want them making the same mistakes I did. As they were getting used to me being home and being part of their lives once again, I had to be patient.

It's tough for a mother or father getting out of prison. We want to do what is right with our children, but we don't know how to handle the rejection. So, for parents who are in this position, we have to understand that it's not going to happen overnight—but we have to remain faithful and stay the course.

I think that may be the problem with parents who get out of prison—they want to make everything right, right away. We want to do right and expect our families to forgive us for our actions. But we must understand that they are also dealing with hurt and trust issues because of our prior choices in life. It will take time for them to allow us back into their lives. We have to be patient. Stay the course. You will see the change.

So now my wife and I had made a commitment to serve the Lord and stay the course. We knew too much was at stake for us to go back to the gang life. We also were now grandparents. Our daughter Jeanette had given birth to our first granddaughter, Angel, in 2005, a few months before I was released. She was about three months old when I got out.

We started attending a local church in Corona. I got a job at a local plastic sheeting company where they hired parolees. It wasn't the greatest job, but it was stable and gave us a chance. I was promoted to a quality control inspector position after only a few weeks of working there. That lasted for a few months or so before I got another job, which I will explain later.

Our youngest son, Albert, was about eleven years old. He was the only one who had joined his mom and I while we were going to church. He got involved in the youth group there, and I had volunteered to help with the youth. I wanted to be there with my son. This was one way we spent time together. We became close as we spent time sharing the Word together. One of my greatest memories with him was when he and I tagged team one of the old neighbors by sharing the Gospel with him. My son told him how Jesus changed my life and could do it for him too. We ended up praying for this guy outside our home. I was so blessed to see my son being used to share the love of Christ.

The change of being home took some adjusting. I had to remind myself daily that it was different being out. I think for me the hardest change for me was adapting to the level of respect people showed to each other. Prison was always about respect. If you got disrespected, you fought. On the outside, it is much different, there is little respect for others. When I saw disrespect, I would immediately want to fight. But then I learned to remind myself that I'm not in prison anymore. I would continually say to myself, *I'm home now.*

# *Chapter 18*

# RESTORATION

As my new life began to take shape, I began to see the results of God's restoration in my life.

After working for about nine months at the plastic sheeting company, my dad and I began talking again. During this time, he was transitioning into a new job too, and he asked me if I wanted to work with him. I prayed about his offer and felt the release from the Holy Spirit to work with him. So, we started the new job together. It was a warehouse job. My dad was the manager and I was supposed to be the warehouse supervisor. However, that never came to fruition.

We worked together for about a year. Together we would load and unload a couple of trucks each week, which gave us time for a lot of catching up on each other's lives. We hadn't talked for several years, so we definitely had a lot of catching up to do. One day he began to revisit our past.

I actually told him, "Dad, you don't need to go there, I really do forgive you." He said that I deserve to know why I was treated differently, so we ended up talking and going back to that place and time and talked about what happened. Then he apologized.

We both sat there with tears in our eyes. For me, even though I had forgiven him in my heart, what I didn't know was that the sting of the pain was still there. Going back to that place brought healing in me, so now not only did I forgive, but healing happened too. It was definitely a divine appointment that we both needed. Now Dad and I really do walk in love for one another. It is an amazing example of God's love for us.

After about a year or so, Dad and I were talking, and he said that the company we worked for might be laying me off, that they were probably going to shut down the warehouse. So I began to look for another job. I called a friend from my church, Jay, and he said to call Carlos, another friend I knew from the church we attended. At the time, I thought Carlos was a manager or supervisor somewhere; I had no idea he had recently opened an engineering company. So I called Carlos and asked if he was hiring. He said to call back a week later. After calling several times and being persistent, and with the help of Jay speaking on my behalf, Carlos finally agreed to bring me aboard.

On December 16, 2007, I started working with Inland Engineering Services (IES), where I would later become a manager. While writing this book, I celebrated eleven years working with IES. I thank God for opening the doors at IES for me. It was there that I grew an understanding of how a business operates and learned how to manage people. These attributes have helped me in pastoring a church that the Lord has called me to lead.

In 2015, Brenda and I were launched out of Goodnews Church to start Kingdom Living Church in Corona, California. We were ordained in 2010 at Goodnews where we served as youth pastors under Pastors Kurt and Mary Schroeder. Of course, my wife and I fought the call to start the ministry—we never wanted to leave Goodnews Church. However, the Lord had other plans.

I recall one occasion when Dr. Dennis Sempebwa came to Goodnews and was ministering there. He called me out and began to prophesy over me. He mentioned that in about two years we would blow up in our ministry, that people would ask where we came from. I had tears rolling down my face, not from happiness, but from anger. I was so upset with the Lord, because we didn't want to leave Goodnews Church. Yet, this wasn't the first time this word from God was spoken over us. It seemed that everywhere we went, the Lord was using people to speak over us about starting a church.

Now we are celebrating four years as a ministry. We are seeing the Lord move among us and use us in ways I never thought possible. Since writing this book, I have started traveling to Africa with Dr. Dennis and his ministry, as well as continuing to pastor Kingdom Living Church.

Despite my small beginnings and poor choices, God has called me to do things that I couldn't do without His hand being upon my life. I'm looking forward to seeing what is next! I'm living with expectation to experience "Kingdom Living." It's not just our church name—it's a way of life. Will you join us? Please do.

# About the Author

Frank Hernandez's beginnings were humble and tumultuous. It is from the mire of abandonment, violence, prison, and addiction that Jesus Christ rescued him.

He has worked as a telecommunication engineering and construction manager and is currently a safety and fleet manager for the same California Telecommunications Contracting Company.

For ten years, Frank has served as a youth pastor and an associate pastor at Goodnews Church in Riverside, California. In 2015, he planted Kingdom Living Church in Corona, California, where he still serves as senior pastor.

He also serves a missionary both domestically and internationally. He is currently completing his formal advanced education with THE 300, a ministry training college.

Frank is married to his beautiful wife of twenty-six years, Brenda Hernandez. They have four children, Andrea, Jeanette, Frank Jr., and Albert. They also have seven grandchildren.

**Get in touch with us:**

**EAGLE'S WINGS INTERNATIONAL**

P O Box 6295, McKinney TX 75071, USA

Email: office@e-wings.net
**www.e-wings.net**

Made in the USA
Columbia, SC
11 August 2020